Christmas at Rockefeller Center

Christmas at Rockefeller Center

Poems by Kirby Olson

CW Books

Published by CW Books

P.O. Box 541106

Cincinnati, OH 45254-1106

ISBN: 9781625491565

LCCN: 2015953034

Poetry Editor: Kevin Walzer

Business Editor: Lori Jareo

Cover design by Riikka Olson. Image of the Christmas Angel, by Valerie Clarebout, is used with permission of Rockefeller Center Archives.

Visit us on the web at www.readcwbooks.com

Contents

Charity is injurious unless it helps the recipient to become independent of it.—John D. Rockefeller

Christmas

Christmas at Rockefeller Center

after Marianne Moore

I, too, dislike it: the requisite Norwegian Spruce,
the hanging of 30,000 ornaments, the mad search
through Saks for the perfect gift. Stuffing oneself
with stuffing. Dressing in scarves and mittens,
venturing out to see the manger at St. Patrick's,

wooden animals, wooden Jesus, red poinsettias.
The city walks together, walks and looks.
There is caroling in whitened streets—some hold
a candle in one hand, some the hand of a child.
I point out the Swarovski star atop the tree,

but something else haunts the scene—a ghost.
Her gypsy resolve beneath five vintage coats,
her ragged clothing and shopping bags,
she is a department store that failed,
lying in the pew with an Eastern European scarf.

Thirty-five feet in radius, the wide berth of her stench.
What mystery is in the shopping bags?
Where are her mother and father? Does she dream
of childhood in a Polish village? In her
we discover, after all, a place for the genuine.

Time after Epiphany

Kairos

the moment
when
the particular

coincides
with the infinite
the moment

she looks
at her watch
and realizes

that our millennium
is over
or that she's late

for brunch
with the mayor
or that she's

on time
for the meeting
with the school board

Trash Night

I walk out with the garbage
under the stars.

                      Wife
usually has to remind me,
but tonight I remembered—
brief silence before I die.

I wonder why we've received no bill
from the collection company
for six months.

                    Daughter
wants to be held when I come back in.
I pick her up, say "Love you."
She asks, "Why, Daddy, why?"
At age three there's still a belief
that there are answers to such things.

I love her because I love her,
because she is Lola, because
when she says *why daddy why*
my heart is an accordion in love
with polka and we do the hokey-pokey
in two step and in three while Tristan
looks out the corner of his eye

                    at us and is happy——but why?

Data from a Doorman

Snow howls in whorls,
about the head of the Statue of Liberty,
about Times Square and the George
Washington Bridge, Harlem,
and in Brooklyn's Prospect Park:
confetti to celebrate the New Year.

As I drink decaf coffee
in the Times Square Marriott, I do
the crossword, and wonder where
the stars such as Bob and Bing
have gone, where the horses
of Central Park and the swans
of Prospect, as snows
accumulate on the Cross Bronx.

I ask the doorman. Snow accretion
is removed by administrative fiat, he says, as
beeping yellow trucks take it to the melters.
Trecan Snow Melters cost a half million dollars.
They can handle eighty tons of snow in an hour.

The melters are less delicate, I think,
than the lettering on an Oreo cookie,
or the elegant curves of the metal on a fire engine,
an index finger in a cool glass of milk,
a model's arm along a walnut banister, or
the quiet of a thread falling in a museum.

As the noisy machines melt the snow,
they push it down the alabaster sewers to treat it,
before releasing it back into the Hudson.
Sixty melters can clear a blizzard in one night:
giving us a New Year's Day that starts out right.

Choice

Beauty's a woman
with a triple nose piercing
in a battered Chevy pick-up.

Outside Family Dollar
she waits while her 18-year-old boyfriend
runs in to buy her a pack of Salem Lights.

He comes back out, thirteen cents short.
She digs in her purse, finds a quarter
with green gum stuck on it,

then feeds organic mango sauce
to the baby she couldn't bear
to abort.

Lent

The Bus

"Poetry is the mother tongue of the human race."
—Georg Hamann

The bus crawls through burbs.
Hungry from fasting.
I read Hamann,
blow bubbles, sleep.
Couples talk about France,
of course.
The bus stinks,
perfume's stale.
I sleep in engine
snores, wake up
three miles past my stop.

The National Trust at Montpelier

"If men were angels, no government would be necessary."
The Federalist Papers, No. 51

The tractors' wheels like Roosevelt dimes
roll over the rills before the Blue Ridge Mountains.
The costs have increased since Jefferson's nickel.
Where slaves ministered to James Madison's fields,
the National Trust is tilling the race course.

Federalists wanted the magistrate to review laws:
legislation that streamlined the administration
and "elevated the level of decision-making"*
to that of a golden quill behind armored fenestration
so we could have Brown vs. Board of Education.

Locomotive at Sunset

Armored battalions among orchids,
Monitor and Merrimac clash amidst crab pastures.
Lincoln quotes Euclid on equality as a proposition

after all the cannons blowing heads off amidst lilies
Minié balls through the wheat fields in the gloaming
a Derringer's bullet (equalizer) finds its mark.

The wounded from Appomattox and Chickamauga
salute their fallen president
amidst industrial landscapes and vast prairies

as the funeral cortege takes him (the lilac)
through Newark, Harlem, and South Chicago,
out to Springfield, to replant him as a sprig.

Orleans Parish

Iron picket fence,
blue-black and proud
as Creole cheekbones,

standing by the sidewalk,
she comes
up and unlocks the church,

her Buick still
emitting exhaust.

Inventiveness

Air wasn't bad, nor light,
and water had endless uses:
baptisms, and for walking on.

When air, light, and water
got together
they formed a rainbow,

a promise. Compare
a man on a cell phone
calling in a mortar strike.

Waiting for the Rapture

While I walked through
the parking lot
where there were many

cars—sick and bulbous,
with sweet frost metal—

a blackbird flew single
through the choleric blush
of street lamps.

Uncertainty

My daughter's hand: Swollen!
The newspaper reports
the disease.

I walk down Second Street,
the police car
going by: Hail!

The policeman waving,
the policeman here to protect
against the television,
the projections of lawlessness.
Christian law versus

Roman uproar. (Yes, Tiberius
slaughtered 50,000
in the Coliseum: Hail!).
The angels, where are the angels, hailing?

Catskills in February

A trail in the snow to a disintegrating trailer,
dying apple trees near the red barns,
a harsh winter day with white-outs:
some think it's time to move on.

There's salt on the roads,
a defective toilet flushing constantly,
old Scotch tape stuck on the window:
some think it's time to move on.

I wear a mix of gloves to shovel snow,
then deal with more dirty dishes.
I still don't know what to do with old Christmas cards.
The snowplow goes by, is it time to move on?

Shoes never worn pile up.
I never fix the uneven picture.
The shadow of a tree on muddy snow.
Everywhere there are empty houses (snowbirds).
I'm chilled to the bone: it's time to move on.

A moosehead over the fireplace, I listen to the fish tank filter,
a rusty pitchfork stands in the mudroom near a dusty
encyclopedia. There are potholes
in the roads, scuff marks on cherry floors.
Tell me about it. It's time to move on.

The TV clicker in hand, I scan the seven o'clock news.
The same complaining, whining voices.
I look out the corner of my eye at the unopened tax
department notice. On the screen, dead Syrians,
the twisted face of the dictator.

Spring's coming and with it the dandelions and tomatoes, returning geese, short skirts, outside barbeque. Let's see each other soon. How about them Yankees?
What's not to like? It's almost spring.

Spirit Boxes

In Kingston, NY, Marilyn Stablein
invited us into her studio, an amazing
old workshop once inhabited
by a men's clothing and accessories outfit.

It's directly underneath the Uptown Bar
which she owns with her husband,
Gary Wilke. My friend Paul and I
were looking at strange white boxes.

Marilyn calls them spirit boxes.
They were boxes like Joseph Cornell's,
but spray-painted white and filled
with children's toys and baseballs and books.

I said, "I'm going to ask you point-blank
what they mean." Marilyn said,
"I don't want to talk about it," and
her eyes began to well with tears.

"Two summers ago, my son
was driving out from California to see me,
when in Lexington, Nebraska, at exit 271,
a truck lost its brakes and rear-ended his car."

Opening Day

for VL

Taking the arched bridge over the Delaware River,
I see the nylon line of a fisherman cast,
as the fly lands in the water and drifts.

It's a musical town:
a fisherman in waders hooks a rainbow trout.

I'm on the way to the optometrist's.
The fog over the town lifts like an opera curtain.
Someone is singing an aria on NPR.

The trout leaps an arc.
In the calm pool, a double rainbow.

Poetry Is for All

A businessman in a Rolls in Manhattan,
a housewife in a Mercedes-Benz in New Paltz,
a beatnik in a paint-splattered VW in Woodstock.

Prose comes by bicycle, horse-drawn carriage,
by Zeppelin, by motorboat, by hang glider.

Poetry prefers to walk.

At the Museum

The circumspect circumlocutions of humbug
that make up the artist's statement
do not equal or rival the red print
of the Magician who could walk on water,

multiply loaves, or gather fish in quantity.
The image of Him on the Cross is
a performance by a lowly carpenter,

lower than Shakespeare,
a performance which completes
that of Moses, who led them out of the desert,
to the green, pleasant fields of Jerusalem.

Decades

I know what it is
to eat a bean
with a plastic spoon
under a dim light,

and to fit together
such small objects,

that is, to join them
with glue.

I know what it is
to watch an eyelid
lift and close and close,
to watch a person
quiver open

as during nervous

    prayer with You.

Easter

Testing God

"It is not good to test your God."
Matthew 4:7

You set out a sheet of black wax paper at age seven
and asked God to sprinkle it with red shavings
to prove His existence.

In the morning, a ladybug walked on the paper.
This was difficult to interpret.

The following night you left out a sheet of pink wax,
and asked God for white shavings.
In the morning, it snowed on the Easter cherries.

One Day I Set Out to Measure

"In those days there was no king in Israel, every man
did that which was right in his own eyes."
Judges 21: 25

I bought a ruler and set out to measure
a cathedral, bottom to top.
I used the shadow of it
and drew its circumference to scale.

What could I not do with ruler, compass,
pencil and paper? I measured
the jump of Jezebel from Jezreel's tower.

Rubbernecking the Margaretville Shooting

"For what is evil but the absence of the good?"
—St. Augustine

We drove to Margaretville
the day after the headlines,
fog clinging to the fields,
a faint purplish blush
brushing the treetops,
through Andes with its
ruined April streets.

We went over the mountain,
past the Sunoco
where the shooter shot a cop
after a routine stop.
We bought licorice
at the candy shoppe.

I grabbed a map
of Delaware County,
looked for Cemetery
Road, where the shots
resulted in two dead,
another trooper and Trim,
the 23-year-old who'd fired
so many rounds out the windows
of a yellow building.

A few cops milled about.
We ate our licorice.
The dealer had been smoked
by New York's Finest.

Saw their gray suits
and striped, brimmed hats
standing before a hole
made by a collapsed house.

April 28, 2007

Remembering Dandelions in Winter

Supervisors ponder budgetary problems.
Snow removal trucks made in Dunn, North Carolina,
have big orange cabs built to last.

The trucks idle county-wide,
As transportation crews spread salt.

Soon, ladybugs helicopter, bluebirds swoop,
dandelions pandemonium new-mown lawns,
as road crews fill potholes with asphalt.

Stewart's: Sunday, May 4, 2003

Mr. Stewart gives our kids harmonicas,
talks about his store.
The counters are a hundred years old,
"Nothing works right,"
and all the fixtures are broken.
Tristan wants out and stands by the door,
Lola wants up in mom's arms.
Riikka thinks the shop historical
as I gaze at compasses and maps.

Now I'm at the corner of Main and Elm
in Oneonta, outside Mama Nina's Pizzeria.
The Blazers are leading the Mavs by two,
cars go by in a dream of motors.
Mr. Stewart has never married—has no family.
The department store is grandfathered,
no one will take over when he closes it.
Now in his late 80s, he talks about the past,
a good listen if you're in no hurry.

Space-Age Suburb Sonnet

Green translucent toothbrush above
sink of white ceramic, spit out
glob of turquoise toothpaste. Rinse
water through teeth, tongue, gums.

My jet-pack! Slip it on,
climb into the sun, like
a scuba diver to your shutters of blue
pink flowerbox. You sleep in a see-through.
Like a clumsy bee I buzz the air up,
to where you nestle in your suburban bed.
You smile, and scream for your dad.

He bats down the door with a rouge bazooka,
fires it at me (misses), then sees us
in pink and vermillion robes
as we kneel and pray to Lord Jesus.

Time after Pentecost

Poetry and Motion

Zeno suggested
the nullity of motion,
that the arrow never hits its mark.

The croquet ball enters a wicket.
The puck slips across ice,
baseball clears a fence,
basketball hits all net.

Into the hands of a tight end
the football spirals.

Goods Damaged in Transit

Whatever happened to the Woman's Christian Temperance Union?

A double-parked *Dos Equis* delivery man on Brooklyn's
Court Street loses control of a pallet of beer
from his forklift. He puzzles as the beer fizzles
from crinkled cans, carbonation spritzes from fissures.

The sobriety of the driver is questionable
as he delivered the means of drunkenness—
ponders whether the pallet was overloaded
at the warehouse, or if the jack malfunctioned.

His Hispanic features wrinkle with consternation
as he wonders whether he tipped too far forward,
if he'll be docked or fired or sent back,
or if the dip from bed to gate was too steep.

A blonde client emerges from the superette
in a periwinkle-print dress. She runs
and simulates a pole dance amidst the misty miasma,
ejaculating a sodden "Hallelujah!"

June 6, 2006, 10:30 a.m.

Jersey (July)

(By the sea, vacancy.)

In the wading pool, a litter
of starfish.

In the surf, a dollar
floating, a green paper fish.

(By the sea, vacancy.)

A prop airplane, alone above Cape May,
alone above the lighthouse, carrying
a ripple-word banner.

Baby, it is easy to push
the beachball at the sea.
Back and forth, forth.

Baby, it's easy to be
at the sea.

(In that vacancy
 by the sea.)

Cousins in Lakes

The shores of Finnish lakes lined with sauna cabins:
since antiquity they have used them for recreation.
Moose in the shallows, their necks above water.

Swimming, laughing, steaming, the Finns
and the moose share the lakes,
rejoicing in farts, and heat, and recreation. Cousins.

The Tornado at Great Escape

Many countries can't get clean water.

Here, thousands of semi-nude citizens
line up willingly to carry clover-leaf rafts
up 75 feet of wood and steel steps to drop
down a polyurethane

                    tunnel into the mouth
                    of
white water (5000 gallons a minute),
a vortex
of Yellow and Blue panels
(Op Art),
then a splash pool
where others retrieve
the raft

            to commence their journey.

It takes hours to arrange

                  on a busy Sunday in July.
It takes five seconds to experience,
as the family (with cousin Siiri) twirls and

                      drops.

Nijinsky's Legacy

Vaslav Nijinsky's missing legs—
belated carnations from the early 20th century.

Our legs take us through summer evenings, lawns, crickets.
Our legs erupt into music as we walk.

Far from the New Jerusalem

Shirts with imprints of red lampposts on blue cloth
clothe the men in the particular city I sing—
women wear pleated red dresses and black

Danskin tops, the very day when the crows glide
with feathers like fingers, the boats in the canal
with their yellow stripes touching the wharf.

The Gold of Time

At the butterfly garden (toward Bovina),
orange monarchs landed on milkweed to dine.
I showed Julian and Tristan the milk in the milkweed.

"Can we eat it?" Tristan asked.
"No," I said, to be safe.
I imagined 10,000 BC, dads
tasting the milkweed before Wikipedia was born.

The kids ran around the bend,
threw rocks in the river.
The monarchs reigned
like Monopoly 500s.

What Is Liberty?

Liberty: it's a notion that grew over 3,000 years.
Moses, Jesus, St. Paul, Magna Carta,
Martin Luther, John Locke:
English, American, French revolutions.

Against it the huddling masses,
yearning to breathe free:
the seaspray against the bronze.

I'd like to step out of my dad suit
and become a non-stinging insect—
lighter than a glider—floating
through New York's orange air,
on my way to the latest restaurant,
where I would land on a platter
and eat for free (too small
to carry a wallet), and helicopter away,
leaving the waitress holding her tray,
a stunned Statue of Liberty.

The Three Wise Men Visit the Guggenheim

A horse pranced proudly
while the wise virgin
wobbled on a trapeze,
her child suspended in gravity
on horseback, arms akimbo.

Jesus on the highwire
in the temple,
He juggled the Trinity,
before the porcine Pilate resorted
to the lion tamer's whip.

Hovering above
the circumambulations
of the unwise builder,
curlicues of spiraling shells amuse,
as circus freaks will.

Still contemplating the conical twists
of Richard Serra, each
marvels at Rouault's depiction
of them at Bethlehem.

Diamonds are a Boy's Best Friend

The sphere is thrown
and its threads revolve.
My boy pops it up.
It's his first time at bat.
The shortstop catches it,
and he's out.

Bees zigzag the diamond.
T's cap has a curvilinear bill
and his shirt says "Braves."
The world spins, orbs shine

in endless complexity.
To infinity and beyond!
Yet here on this diamond,
nine face nine in the first

game of their lives
and the oscillation of the spinning orb
holds parents and grandparents
in the levity of its gravity.

Pax Americana

I remember the Americans in Paris that summer,
how they walked in high socks and neat shorts, their hair
combed, looking brainless as dolls.

My friend, a Frenchman, pointed to them.
They were in couples, and he said,
"What are they, who are they," laughing,

and they dawdled on, with their cameras.
They'd come from Oklahoma. They were real people.
They knew they had not come from the earth

and that they would not return to dirt, and they pointed out
buildings to their little nodding son.
These Americans. They eat spaghetti and clip

their fingernails before badminton, so they don't cut
their thumbs on the upswing. They read the newspaper
just for the funnies, for the rest surely is wrought of lies.

They shop around before they buy, because it could be cheaper
somewhere else. They have honest intercourse, and have
simplified their fourscore to a few two-kingdom ideas.

Bang for a buck, yup. They cut the line at Notre Dame,
in through the side door, past the lines heaving in the heat.
They looked at the great violet halo of the North Transept.

How they looked!

The Romantic World

The topography of the world is diverse:
there are canyons, rivers, a skyscraper or two.
Once there were many romantic volcanoes.
In the ocean are old fish reading books about tropical fish.

The oldest fish is less than fifty thousand years old.
There is a country on earth whose name is Romania,
where taste runs to opera and short romantic novels.
A Romanian invented the gadget for making ice cubes.

Later in his life he retired to a tributary of the Amazon,
high up in the clear air of mountainous Peru.
He was the leader of a clan who worshipped tropical fish.
There are newspapers, and every now and then an ocean liner
sinks

provoking five-inch headlines, and later, short romantic novels.
Isn't it curious, even romantic, that turtles still exist?
The pace of the world quickens, yet turtles thrive.
There used to be a lot of good romantic operas written every
year.

Perhaps the best one was by Wagner and is called the Ring.
His own life could be the subject of a romantic opera,
as is often the case: a composer's art mirrors his life.
Also, the way a composer dies is often a strange summary

of the way a composer lived. Everybody on earth's life
is a good subject for a romantic opera, but I doubt
any more good romantic operas will be written.
Composers are no longer concerned with the world.

The Triangular Root of the Sphere

A ladybug helicopters over the grapefruit basket,
frost on the grass in November,
Orion's belt on a moonless night.
The shimmer of a mirage over the desert at sunset.
Two white birds flying together at first light.

An arcing, twirling long bomb for a touchdown,
a strike to close the last frame on a perfect game,
a swish from the top of the key with .2 left,
a whale surfaces in Puget Sound against the Olympics.
A hawk wheels over a pine forest in the Poconos.

Metro North Rider

Hat off in the train,
he reads *Green Door,*
as landscape rolls
by the window.

He rides in a blue and gray passenger car.

He sees a cow in a marigold field
standing beside a white church,
and his binoculars follow the cow
as he notes in his diary, "Dairy."

E = Times Squared

Gliding gaily through the grid,
the electrons rejoice at the illumination
they offer. Times Square
is the energy of the masses

brought into a squared
concatenation of color

to advertise the photovoltaic cell
which underlies so many

electrical contrivances since Edison.
Today everyone marvels

at the news of the new brought
to them via the networks;

you see mega-stars whose electricity
is undeniable drop dead almost
simultaneously, stop and stare, and you
will come ever closer to the scandalous

spectacularity of the photon like a cow
mooning the stars, as Gandolfini joins
Andromeda and Orion, leaving us
perplexed at the lightness of being.

Fireflies inside a jar,
the headlights of a car,
a war sped on by searchlights,
the hope to dronemeisters

offered by the radar.
None eclipse the lightswitch,

that gives us mastery over the
electron: all hail its power!

The atom is the bomb.

Reading Adam Smith at Halloween

"…he intends only his own gain, and he is in this,
 as in many other cases, led by an invisible hand."
The Wealth of Nations, Adam Smith

They came to the door,
princesses in pink,
cowboys in corduroy,
aliens in silk pajamas,
ninjas in nighties.
We gave them 100 Grand Bars.

The mechanical reproduction
of the masquerade
turns crook into cook,
space ranger into forest ranger,
mutates carnival children
into garbage collectors,
automobile repairmen,
nurses, construction foremen,
doctors, lawyers, infantry men:
all part of capitalist induction.

James Ensor's *Christ's Entry
Into Brussels in 1889*
posits a carnival for adults
with God lost amidst
the commercial tumult.

In Greenwich Village,
adults get in touch
with their monstrous children
as accountant becomes pirate,
advertising exec hooker,
postal worker skeleton
bringing dead letters to Bartleby.

Advent

Proprietary Title

The rind of a melon, the rind of a lemon.
The soft skin of a tomato versus a pineapple.
These are like the watermelon or the ugli fruit,
unequivocally, like the potato, or the orange—
or the apple, which Eve ate.

A sermon on Creation summons envelopes
to the plate, as the pastor asks, "What is Life?"
The torn cover of a baseball, a Zeppelin exploding
over Berlin, the moon craters
of a golf ball, the lid on a jar of Clamato—

all of those are copyrightable,
but the superstructure of the plum is God's.
The judge bangs her gavel as she moves
to resolve what's in hundreds of articles:
the dispute between Monsanto, et al,
over whether all forms can be owned. She

argues that forms which reproduce
on their own are life, whereas those requiring
industrial production are not. Thus, the debate
over the pomegranate is concluded by the magistrate.

Adam's Family

In the garden as imagined by Edward Hicks,
the lion lay down with the lamb.
Humans ate fruit. Of the fruit marked

"Don't eat," a snake hissed *Help yourself.*

So out the west gate into dissonance,
the gnashing of teeth, twelve tribes,
a dispersal into war and pestilence.
To offset the dispersal into pestilence

the mercantilization of divine citrus,
and then the myth of an apple a day.
Today there are 7,500 varieties.

Autumn in Delhi

Every morning the fog bunches along the Delaware.
This morning the fog clings to the mountain.
The fog is about to burn off, revealing infinity,
as a last butterfly hovers over the barren garden.
It is warm today—perhaps I should plant garlic.

Clouds float over, as do turkey vultures.
The autumn foliage contrasts with the rising mist.
The Victorian and Queen Anne houses
have pumpkins on their porches, with black cats
that sit near them. They watch the dogs.

Red and purple bruised leaves lack chlorophyll.
My son Julian says the only word that rhymes
with orange is orange. One is the fruit
and the other is the color.
My daughter

and I watch a crow soar up the valley. Crows
are a murderous confederation. They walk
hands behind their backs on telephone lines,
as if funereal lawyers, cawing
about wills and trusts, depositions, insisting

on the redistribution of goods from one generation
to the next. Quoth the Raven: Nevermore!
I teach Sofia to count to five
using her toes and fingers, as somewhere in Florida
a thousand flamingos ascend from the Everglades.

November

Rock fences litter Delaware County.
Driving, one sees smoke curl from chimneys
into necklaces of geese gone south.

The town is empty at six a.m.
A lone bundle of clothes
waits at the red light to cross,
steam pouring from her mouth.

Brooklyn Bridge

Laid end to end,
it has the segmentation of the Eiffel,
connecting the two largest cities
into one megalopolis for megalomaniacs.

If you can't make it there,
it doesn't mean you can't make it anywhere.
Perhaps you'd have been better off
in Delhi before the Civil War,

with a wad of milkspun money
while the financing of the Brooklyn Bridge
was being arranged by Tammany,
who'd Shanghai'd the top hats and dancing,

and released a flurry of three-dollar bills,
junk bonds—"made it there"
while white birds filled the air and businessmen
read their watches and fingered their hair.

Solzhenitsyn

"Over a half century ago, while I was still a child, I recall
hearing a number of old people offer the following
explanation for the great disasters that had befallen Russia:
**'Men have forgotten God; that's why all this has
happened…'"** –Solzhenitysn

If I were to write poems
like a train on parallels to Siberia, past
onion domes, aspiring jazz stars,
in samizdat basements,
zigzags of proletarian taxis, busy streets,
lunches including inexpensive meats,
smuggled ouzo,
would I write every poem
that is forbidden to exist?

Snow falls beside abandoned cathedrals.

Serving Time

Time is a beautiful old woman with long salt and pepper hair.
Time is as yellow as a Korean newspaper.
It is an accordion wheezing memories of Kim Jong-il.

Time follows money around the track.
Time has fallen like a rider from a monumental horse.
Zebras referee the silence at the prison dinner

for those whom the calendar has forgotten,
whose hair whitens in North Korean prisons.

Molotovs and Mazeltovs

for Riikka

The sleighbells ding in the Finnish forest.
Horses race through the wintry lace.

Marriage is a trace of the prefecture
in the unity of paradise.

Shape Is Determinant of Meaning

Eggs are ovals
and cars flutter by on wings.
Trash cans are cylindrical.
Basketballs are spherical.
Stars are pointy like starfish.

Nobody knows the eyes are stars.
The sweet, warm weather in her sweater.
Everything that I know indicates
that the truth shall be known.
A square shall become a triangle.

The Chapel

"Be fruitful."
Genesis 9:1

The hurt people gathered
to put their noses against the glass
and look within.

Columbus walked like a beetle across
the plum, and set out across the Atlantic,
his head tilted to one side and his heart
to the other, listening to Isabella and Ferdinand.

The mercantilization of citrus followed,
the orange groves that had already sucked
the Middle East dry had now alighted upon
Florida, and once in, no one could stop
the orchards.

Who's Counting?

To peel an orange into sections is bizarre—
there are always thirteen sections—
the twelve disciples, plus the Lord,
the seeds of eternal life.

The Romans Versus the Trinity

With their aqueducts,
their gladiator contests,
their bridal chambers,

Nero and Caligula,
Tiberius and Seneca,

they hadn't any morals as such—
a few rights for the privileged.

The slaves were mere furniture,
broken and thrown into the cemetery
like everyone else, including the emperor.

St. Paul argued that a new god was afoot.
Mercy, love, charity, faith.
The meek would inherit the earth.
For a culture that believed in canaries inside of pigs
so that the chef could startle the emperor
with marvelously unsanitary whims
leading to barfatoriums,
the coming of St. Paul from the provinces
must have seemed a rude joke.

Paul's head bounced thrice upon decapitation.
The triangle rang the Trinity.
Zeus and Hades, hushed.

Mathematical Calculations

for Stu

What is left of time?
Subtraction
is the melody of God
as we disappear,
only to reappear—
the trickle of kingdoms
in a sand clock.

Bodies in Motion Tend to Stay in Motion

Running Lola to the crossroads
as steam caresses the frozen hills
and water trickles the creases.

The soft pink light of the sun
caresses the craggy trees
as cars ease around icy curves.

A crow in the distance hulks
as its wings flap—
a comma moving toward a period.

Ancient Catskills

Pterodactyls flew over the campus
on the leathery wings of 340 million years ago.
Where I grade students with bloody ink,

Tyrannosaurus fought in the ferns.
Leviathans plunged in a sea the size of Manhattan
where today wasps crawl under rural eaves.

Giant beaver tangled with saber-toothed tigers.
The darkening of the sedges
on the edges of the meadows

accompanies the coming of winter:
I think of forests of mastodonts running –
they've lost their white gloves in the library.

Stars in the Early Morning

Their names are grown obscure:
Andromeda, Cassiopeia, Orion.
Each is an aria of disaster.

The power of the Testament is not to any
physical body, nor to any particular person,
as Paris had found his heaven in Helen.

His sisters raped and murdered by Greeks,
father stabbed on the throne,
brother Astyanax thrown from ruins.

Diogenes looked in vain with his lamp, but
Jesus was able to find humanity in the faces
of the obscure people who lived in byways.

Thaw

I put on my gloves and went
to the car that took me
through infinity to work,
through the oscillations of weather,
through glittering streets of lace
(the snow fell from above).

As I worked,
the car door froze shut,
and when it came time to quit
it was stuck.

Kevin at Groundskeeping
threw a bucket of warm water on the door,
the lock clicked open,
and I drove home again through infinity,
took off my gloves

and said hello to my loves.

The Mercantilization of Christmas

From the 7th floor rusted cars trudge.
The wintry streets of Delhi look clean.
The light at Main and Kingston changes.

Police lights revolve to take down a speeder.
Citizen going too fast with costly gasoline,
I stick out my tongue like a parking meter

as they pass. Over the Delaware River fog,
crows as boomerangs in the treetop firs.
Coldness in the unlit corridors at work.

I've popped in for cookies from the Christmas party.
Flies crinkled on the table around the cookie plate.
Twinkling lights illuminate the crooked legs.

Capitalism as the parable of the talents:
wise men bearing frankincense, myrrh, and gold.
Mary Magdalene's gift of spikenard. Her sense

of His penance is as apparent as theirs.
"But me ye have not always."
His absence her prescience; our present His presence.

Acknowledgements

Some of these poems have previously appeared in *Academic Questions, Aethlon, Agate, Ancient Paths, Asylum, Blast Furnace, Christianity and Literature, Chronicles, Chronogram, Cortland Review, First Things, Green Door, Huffington Post, Light Year, LuzMag, Partisan Review, Passager, Poetry East, Poetry Macau, Potomac Review, RealPoetik, Quarterly Review, Simul: An Anthology of Lutheran Poetry, South Dakota Review, Telephone, Watershed Post, The Wolf, Wordsmith*, and in a chapbook entitled *Waiting for the Rapture* (Rhode Island: Persistencia).

The following poets offered substantive ideas for amendments to certain poems in this manuscript: Aaron Belz and Bryan Roth.

Kirby Olson studied poetry with Gregory Corso and Allen Ginsberg in the late 1970s at Naropa Institute. He lives in the western Catskills with his wife Riikka and their four children.

In addition to poetry, he has published *Temping,* a novel, at Black Heron Press (2005), and several volumes of literary criticism on figures such as Gregory Corso and Andrei Codrescu.

He is a member of AARP and of the Lutheran church in Delhi, NY. He teaches philosophy and mythology and other humanities courses at SUNY-Delhi.

Note

In the poem "The National Trust at Montpelier," the phrase
"elevated the level of decision-making," was used by
Professor Gordon Wood of Brown University during a
conference on Liberty held on Saturday, October 29, 2011.
Wood was paraphrasing the philosophy of James Madison
and the Federalists with regard to the Judiciary. Madison
wanted well-educated persons to make the more important
decisions for the country. Madison did not want the hoi
polloi "with mud on their boots," as Professor Wood put it,
to have too much input. Wood justified this by saying that
otherwise the Brown family would not have been able to
appeal to more vertical elements than the Board of
Education. Wood saw this as obvious, and said that Madison,
too, would have seen the necessity of a Platonic ruler to
chastise the masses, who would otherwise remain mired in
ignorance.

CPSIA information can be obtained at www.ICGtesting.com
Printed in the USA
BVOW08s0946241115

428238BV00001B/1/P